The Invisible Woman

Also by

NICOLE JOHNSON

Fresh Brewed Life
Fresh Brewed Life Study Guide

Keeping a Princess Heart, In a Not-So-Fairy-Tale World
Keeping a Princess Heart - A Conversation Guide for Women

TRILOGY ON FAITH, HOPE, AND LOVE

Raising the Sail
Stepping into the Ring
Dropping Your Rock

NICOLE JOHNSON LIVE (VIDEOS)

Funny Stuff Woman Can Relate To
Stepping into the Ring
There's No Place Like Hope

www.nicolejohnson.net

The Invisible Woman

by

NICOLE JOHNSON

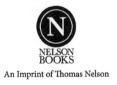

NELSON
BOOKS

An Imprint of Thomas Nelson

Published in Nashville, Tennessee, by Nelson Books, an imprint of Thomas Nelson. Nelson Books and Thomas Nelson are registered trademarks of HarperCollins Christian Publishing, Inc.

Thomas Nelson, Inc., titles may be purchased in bulk for educational, business, fundraising, or sales promotional use. For information, please email SpecialMarkets@ThomasNelson.com.

Scripture quotations, unless otherwise indicated, are taken from *Holy Bible, New Century Version*®. © 1987, 1988, 1991 by Thomas Nelson, Inc. All rights reserved.

Cover Design: Tobias' Outerwear for Books, www.tobiasdesign.com
Page Design: Blackbird Design, www.blackbird-design.com

ISBN 978-0-7180-7921-5 (trade paper)

Library of Congress Cataloging-in-Publication Data

Johnson, Nicole, 1966–
    The invisible woman / by Nicole Johnson.
      p. cm.
Summary: "Nicole Johnson shows how being in the background of others' lives isn't necessarily less important"—Provided by publisher.
Includes bibliographical references.
    ISBN 978-0-8499-1829-2 (tradepaper)
    1. Johnson, Nicole, 1966- 2. Christian biography—United States. I. Title.
    BR1725.J624A3 2005
    242—dc22

2005000302

Printed in the United States of America
15 16 17 18 19 20 LSI 9 8 7 6 5 4 3 2 1

Dedication

FOR MY SISTER VANESSA,

THE MOST BEAUTIFUL INVISIBLE WOMAN

I'VE EVER BEEN ABLE TO SEE

Contents

1.

Chapter One

Now you see me . . .

Now you don't

Now you see me ...
Now you don't

It started to happen gradually . . .

I would walk into a room and no one would notice. I would say something to my family, like, "Turn the TV down, please." And nothing would happen. Nobody would get up or even make a move for the remote. I would stand there for a minute, and then I would say again, a little louder, "Would someone turn the TV down?" Nothing. Finally, in frustration I would go over and turn it down myself.

One day I was walking my son Jake to school. I was holding his hand, and we were about to cross the street when the crossing guard said to him, "Who is that with you, young fella?"

"Nobody," he shrugged.

Nobody? The crossing guard and I laughed. My son is only five, but as we crossed the street I thought, *Oh my goodness, nobody?*

Then I began to notice these kinds of things more and more, because it wasn't only with the kids. I was in the grocery store looking for Fruity Pebbles. A clerk from the store walked by and I said, "Excuse me, but could you . . ." and he was gone. He walked right past me to help a woman further down the aisle, who was having trouble finding extra-fine sugar. She looked about twenty-two and just so happened to be extra fine herself. I was left on my own with the cereal hunt.

Another night my husband and I were at a party. We'd been there for about three hours and I was ready to leave. I noticed he was talking to a friend from work. So I walked over, and when there was a break in the conversation, I whispered, "I'm ready to go when you are." He just kept right on talking, and he didn't even turn toward me or notice that anyone was standing there.

That's when I started to put all the pieces together. I don't think he

can see me. I don't think *anyone* can see me.

I'm invisible.

It all began to make sense—the blank stares, the lack of response, the way someone will walk into the room while I'm on the phone and ask to be taken to the store. Inside I'm thinking, *Can't you see I'm on the phone?* Obviously not. No one can see if I'm on the phone, or cooking, or sweeping the floor, or even resting, because no one can see me at all. I could stand on my head in the corner and inevitably someone would wonder, out loud, "Is my soccer jersey clean?"

I'm invisible.

When I put dinner on the table, everyone acts like it just appeared from nowhere. The four of us can sit down with a full meal in front of us, and Jake will say, "I didn't want milk," as if he's talking to the air. It's the same air that my husband talks to when he surveys the table laden with food and says, "There's no butter." I have come to understand that this means, "I can't see you; I'm not even addressing you. But when I say there is no butter, the butter lady will get up and get it."

And he's right. Presto, the butter appears like magic; the milk gets swapped for juice; and we go on with dinner. No one says thank you, because no one sees that anyone did anything.

My family has no clue how their socks get back in their drawers, how their favorite treats end up in that mysterious brown bag that sits by the door waiting to be picked up on their way out, who comes to pick them up after school, or why the dog doesn't wet on the rug anymore.

Tim, my teenager, takes everyone else's advice but mine. My husband Michael talks to other people like he's interested in the minute details of their lives, yet he doesn't even ask me about my day. My kindergartner wants to play, but my body is just a mountain to roll over with his trucks. I'm nobody. In a crowded room, no one looks me in the eyes. In the grocery store, I'm just a mother in sweats, like every other mother, looking for the on-sale, now sold-out Fruity Pebbles. At a business dinner, I'm just another wife, like every other wife there—a woman who tried to find something nice to wear and is happy to be out of the house. I'm invisible.

Is this what comes from seventeen years of marriage and two children?

My name is Charlotte Fisher, but does it even matter? Mostly I'm just Mom or Honey, the butter lady or the driver. Sometimes I'm "Would you mind?" or "Whenever you get a minute . . ." I also go by "While you're up" or "Since you're going out anyway . . ."

Even the dog doesn't see me. We have a four-year-old mostly beagle named Bonnie. This is especially hard because Bonnie is invisible in our family also. She is shoved aside for better toys, pulled around the neighborhood, and generally ignored since she lost her cute puppy status. For a while I thought maybe we had an understanding between us, but she blatantly broke it the other day. She looked directly at me and peed right on the rug. She never took her eyes off me while she was doing it. The brazen beagle!

At first I didn't care about being invisible. I thought maybe it was just a temporary condition, but the longer it persisted, the harder it became to deal with, because the more I poured myself into my family, the more invisible I became. It was the complete opposite effect of what I was used to. In college or in the workplace, the harder I tried and the

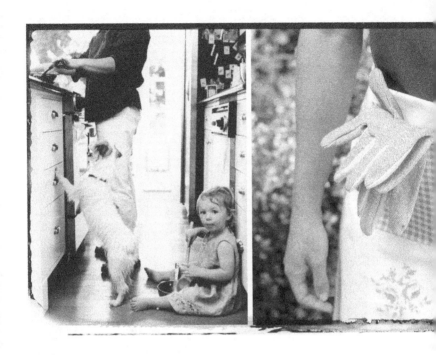

more I gave, the more I had to show for it. I became more visible, not less. But in my house the more I do, the more it gets taken for granted. If I make breakfast three days in a row and skip the fourth day, nothing happens. There is a collective family shrug and no one seems to care one way or another.

It's definitely the law of diminishing—or vanishing—returns: the more I do, the less they see. I'm half afraid they will take all that I have to give and half afraid they won't take anything. On the bad days, when I find myself giving so much in hopes of making them see me, I probably should worry less about being invisible and more about being dead from exhaustion.

I have often wondered when my kids walk into the kitchen if they just see a pair of hands cooking a meal. Maybe I'm like the white-gloved Hamburger Helper hands. Or do they see an apron tied around an invisible waist standing over the stove? When I'm driving the car, do they see an empty seatbelt secure and tight across no one's lap? They can see the trappings of the function I am performing, but they cannot

see me performing it. I can be standing over the stove with tears running down my cheeks, and someone will come into the kitchen and ask "the apron" the inevitable question: not, "What's wrong?" but "What's for dinner?"

Some days I'm only a pair of hands, nothing more.

"Can you fix this?"

"Can you tie this?"

"Can you open this?"

"Can you wash this?"

"Can you hold this?"

Weren't these the same hands that held books, went to college, and even received a law degree? Didn't they grasp and shake the hand of the president of the United States on a college trip to Washington? Are they not the hands that studied piano for five years to be able to play a Bach cantata? Whatever they were, they are now just used for opening video games and washing underwear, making bologna sandwiches and holding a fistful of GI Joes while someone goes to the bathroom.

Some days I'm not even a pair of hands; I'm not even a human being.

I'm a clock to ask, "What time is it?'

I'm the TV guide to answer, "What comes on after this?"

I'm a car to order, "Be there at 5:30!"

Yes, it's true; these were the hands that held books and the eyes that studied history and the mind that graduated summa cum laude—and now they have disappeared into the peanut butter, never to be seen again. I've been reduced to a pair of hands or a clock, and probably a cuckoo clock at that. Can I really say I studied law for this? *She's going . . . she's going . . . she's gone!*

Sometimes when I get together with friends from college or law school, I hear them chatter on about their work, and I can never see my way clear to jump into the conversation. My job is not nearly as exciting as theirs, unless you count the research of what happens to various objects as they cycle through the dryer. My friends might discuss a major court case and my mind goes to precedent on the pillowcase. I won that one just yesterday. One friend brought up the changes in the market,

and my mind pictured a diaper change in the supermarket. I don't think I'll bring up either as my contribution to the conversation.

They have power lunches; I have Power Ranger lunches. Why does

one seem very important and the other, not so? Is it just the nature of women to want what we don't have? Would any of the women at the power lunches trade every entrée on the menu for a peanut butter sandwich with their own little boy? Funny, they rarely say so.

Many days I think it doesn't matter what I do, so I can do anything I want. Irresponsibility comes with invisibility. Why should I be responsible when my family refuses to see me? Responsibility rests on recognition, which is an agreement of sorts. And we do not seem to agree that I exist as a person.

If I am just a role or a function, an apron or a clock, why should I worry about my heart or my tone or my spirit? Clocks don't have spirits. Aprons don't have tones. And a function doesn't get its feelings hurt. What good does a heart do when all you are is an apron?

I feel like a missing person that no one will miss. I am the only one who would notice my picture on the back of a milk carton. No one would ever file the report wondering where I have gone, because they would never know I left. Like a cruel game of hide-and-seek, no one

would come looking for me, and not knowing when to come out, I could die in the place I have been hiding.

My appearance certainly doesn't matter, at least not to anyone else. If I put on a nice dress or cut arm holes into a gunnysack and poke my head through, I always look "fine." Even with all my effort, I've rarely dipped below nor risen above "fine."

Plastic surgery suddenly looks much more appealing. With television makeover shows and reality TV surgeries, it presents itself as the grandest solution to stopping your disappearance. Women are crazy about it because they have the same fear I do. They don't want to fade away—perfect eyes and smooth skin say, "Notice me—I'm still here!" Time, worry, and responsibility have all conspired to make me invisible with wrinkles and creases, but no! Smooth out the wrinkles and suck out the fat so I don't disappear into the world of normal-looking women who no longer turn anybody's head.

When a girl grows up being admired for how she looks, how unbearable it must be when people no longer "see" her. But surely that's

not me! Am I afraid that my husband doesn't value the inside me more than the outside me? To be honest, I'm not sure he values any of me, inside or out. Invisible is invisible. I have actually thought that if my husband can't see me, maybe I should find one who can. But then, that's a different show on another night of the week. Note to self: stop watching television.

I mean, is this what I signed on for? What did I really expect? When you get pregnant, people tell you that you're going to gain weight. Shouldn't someone tell you that you're going to wake up one day in the middle of a marriage and two kids and feel as if your life has suddenly vanished? Shouldn't you be warned that a toddler and a teenager and a husband all have giant erasers, and that even though they don't mean to, they will use them to make you disappear from the paper of your life?

Shouldn't someone have told me that when I ask my husband which shoes I should wear to a special dinner, he is going to say, "Just put something on and let's go; nobody is going to notice your shoes"? That way I wouldn't end up in a crying puddle because no one cares about my

THE INVISIBLE WOMAN

shoes—not even the one person who had a remote chance of caring. I could have been a little more prepared for that giant eraser taking another swipe at a tiny detail, but it was a detail that just might have assured me that I still belong to a grown-up world where shoes matter to people.

Maybe someone did tell me these things, but youth was an anesthetic that numbed my mind, making me believe it could never happen to me. But now it has. Did it happen because me, the real me, the full me, just isn't good enough to be seen anymore? Am I no longer attractive, or fun, or even worth listening to?

Feeling invisible has brought out very strange feelings of jealousy. I feel a little desperate to convince myself that I really do exist in the real world and that I really am a part of all that is going on around me, even when it feels as if I'm not. I have never been jealous before, but if Michael can't see me, then I don't want him to be able to "see" anyone else. If I have to suffer from his blindness, I don't want to hear about some woman at work who doesn't. And I don't want to hear about

Bob's wife Carol, and how great she is with her kids. Does that mean Michael doesn't think I'm good with our kids? How can he compliment Carol when he can't compliment me? If he doesn't see me, why does he see Carol?

Sometimes I play games. If the bathroom lady doesn't clean the toilet, will anyone notice? How bad can it get before someone says something or notices? The answer is *really* bad. If the kitchen lady doesn't place food on the table at six-thirty, will anyone really care? If no one calls them to dinner, will they just willingly starve? They won't starve, but they won't miss having dinner together either. I feel stuck in an endless repetition of events in which I'm powerless to change the outcome. I am living the movie *Groundhog Day* over and over. Nothing I do seems to make a difference to anyone. I know in my mind that this isn't true, but some days, just as in the movie, I want to see how far I can push it and whether or not anything I do matters.

I gained weight—not a lot, just fifteen pounds or so—and no one cared. The earth didn't stop rotating, and my husband even seemed to

understand. Then I lost weight, and no one seemed to care about that either. My kids didn't pay any more attention to me skinny than they did when I was fat. My husband didn't seem more interested in me physically, so I picked fat. If no one could see me, why in the world did it matter? Why not just sit in the Lazy Boy recliner and cultivate my relationship with Reese's Peanut Butter Cups?

One afternoon Tim walked into the kitchen and ate the other half of a sandwich that I had not yet finished. Since he's a teenager, he's a human vacuum cleaner anyway, but he didn't even question whose it was, why it was sitting there on the counter, or whether it was okay to help himself to it. I just watched him wolf it down. He never acknowledged my presence or saw me standing there.

When he turned to go, I stuck my foot out. I'm not sure what I intended to do except to put some obstacle in his path, to slow him down on his way toward taking something else that didn't belong to him. I was going to say, "That was my sandwich, and I wasn't finished with it!" but he went flying over my foot and tumbled into the living

The Invisible Woman

room. He got up looking dazed and confused. I would have laughed, but his eyes registered a touch of hurt.

"Good grief, Mom," he said, "why did you trip me? I didn't even see you there."

"I'm sorry, son," I said, rushing over. "I didn't mean to trip you."

"Then why did you stick your foot out like that?" he questioned, rubbing the carpet burn that was reddening his elbow. At that point the sandwich didn't matter anymore. He didn't see me, so he ate it. Still, I never want to use the invisibility that hurts me to hurt them. Even an invisible person can leave visible wounds.

Then one day I was dropping Jake off at Gloria's house. She is an elderly woman who baby-sits for me and several other families one day a week. I was walking to my car in Gloria's driveway when John, one of our neighbors, called out to me.

"Charlotte!" His smile was friendly and warm, and I waved. He walked over with genuine enthusiasm to speak to me. He's a well-established doctor in our area, and it turns out that he's newly divorced.

Twenty minutes later I realized that I had talked to John longer and enjoyed it more than ever before. I was drawn to him. I liked the way he said my name, and the way he asked me caring questions about how I was doing, and especially the way he looked at me as I answered. I got in my car a little weak in the knees. I felt a little adrenaline rush and a tiny thrill of excitement.

Twenty seconds later, I was scared by the thoughts going through my head. For the first time I thought I needed to get some help.

I decided on lunch with Janice. She's one of my closest friends, and a woman that I would hate if I were immature. She's classically beautiful, wears a size four, and is smart enough to have started her own million-dollar company. She's definitely the kind of woman other women make up reasons not to like, but she's genuinely good to the core. Not that she is without problems, but she has a great perspective on life, and she has the maturity to keep private things private. She was about to take a two-week vacation to Europe, but we squeezed in lunch the day before she left.

From iced tea and bread through the last bite of chocolate torte, we talked nonstop. Toward the end of the meal, I brought up this issue of invisibility, and then I poured my heart out. I realized that although I was only beginning to say it out loud, I had been feeling it for a long time. The feelings came gushing out like water from a broken pipe. What had been an unconscious struggle for self-definition had finally become conscious.

I knew Janice would understand, even if she couldn't relate to my particular situation. I didn't think she would see me as spoiled or self-centered, but I was hoping she would tell me if she did. Instead, she told me that I was just putting into words the feelings we've all felt so many times. I was describing the sadness we all feel in the deepest parts of our hearts, she explained. The isolation. The alienation. The aloneness.

Then she said, "Charlotte, you are asking a question that only you can answer for yourself. The question is *Do I matter?* No one can answer for you. Your kids cannot give you meaning; your husband cannot make your life count. Only *you* can find where the meaning comes from—no one else can do it for you. It's a deep question that has to be settled in the

core of who you are, not by what is going on around you. You have doubts about yourself, so you think that everyone else must have doubts about you too."

I should have offered to write her a check for two hours of therapy, but I bought her lunch instead. Driving home, so many questions rattled around in my head.

Is this fear of invisibility really all about some kind of confusion with my identity as a woman?

Does every woman wonder, Am I really doing the right thing?

Am I spending my life well?

Does this come from complex changes in our culture? Or has it been this way since that dumb apple?

I really didn't know.

It is both irresistible and dangerous to think that other women have it better than I do, that their husbands care more than mine—maybe even help them pick out their shoes! When I see a woman in the grocery store, I can write her life in my head and start to believe it. If her husband

is walking around the grocery store with her, I immediately write him to be a caring and sensitive, I'll-help-you-in-every-way-I-can kind of man.

Then I think about my husband, who is at home watching television, and I write my own life as the underappreciated grocery buyer, coupons in hand, wandering up and down the aisles trying to save a few cents that no one cares about but me. Later I become the family accountant, up late at night with my calculator for company, tracking all the money I've saved, writing checks for bills, trying to balance our budget. I feel like Bob Cratchit in Dickens' *Christmas Carol*, crouched over his ledgers in the lonely corner of a candlelit room. I spiral right down at the speed of light into a bottomless chasm of self-pity. The story of my life ends tragically, with my dying alone and unloved.

Oh puhleeeese! Okay, I know it's not true, but that's the way it feels sometimes.

The conflict with invisibility is comic and tragic. I can laugh and cry at almost the very same time. It's funny and silly on some days when it's so obvious that you just have to laugh. But it is also terribly sad. I feel

stuck in this strange little aspect of the human condition with no plan of escape. It seems there is plenty of medication to help not feel it, but nothing strong enough to cure it.

But sometimes, like after that great lunch with Janice, I feel better. It's good just being able to articulate my feelings and to laugh and cry about the tension. Besides, deep inside, I know that Janice is right. I know that I'm going to have to answer for myself that deep question—
Do I matter?

2.

~ Chapter Two ~

The Divine

Disappearance

chapter two

The Divine
Disappearance

A couple of weeks later a few of us were going over to a little get-together at Janice's house. Everyone loves going to Janice's. Her home is beautiful and always so peaceful—maybe because she doesn't have any children. Apparently she'd had a fabulous trip to England and France, and there were pictures to see and stories to tell.

I loved seeing the freedom Janice and her husband had to travel and enjoy life, but that particular night I couldn't help but think that by the time I get my own life back, it will probably be too late to enjoy it. I wasn't in such a good mood. Michael got home late from work and I couldn't leave until we discussed an issue about Jake's teacher. So I

pulled up to Janice's home, late again, wearing a very wrinkled blouse, car-applied lipstick, and a dirty-hair ponytail. I wasn't in the best frame of mind to see pictures of the English countryside, nor any countryside for that matter.

But as usual, once you get there, being with friends makes everything better. I was able to relax soon after arriving; the cares of home took their proper place in the background; and we all had a very nice evening.

As I was leaving, Janice excused herself to walk me out to my car. As we crossed the lawn she mentioned how much our lunch conversation had stayed with her on her trip. I started to laugh and apologize that my insecurities had followed her across the pond, but she didn't let me finish before she handed me a beautifully wrapped book.

"I knew the minute I saw this," she said, "that I had to bring it home for you." She gave me a quick hug, whispered, "Hang in there!" and headed back to her guests inside.

I drove home wondering what kind of book she'd brought me. I arrived to a sleeping house and a sink full of dirty dishes. I unwrapped

my thoughtful friend's present and found myself looking at a book about the great cathedrals of Europe. The photo on the outside was an absolutely breathtaking picture of sunlit stained glass on Notre Dame Cathedral. I was very curious as I opened the book. I saw Janice's familiar scrawled handwriting and read her inscription: "With admiration for the greatness of what you are building, when only God sees."

I felt a little sting of a tear as I climbed the stairs for bed. Michael was already snoring; so there was no talking to him. Besides it was already pretty late. I set the book on my bedside table and just stared at the cover. The great cathedrals? I appreciated the book, but now I wasn't so sure she'd fully understood our conversation. I was a little embarrassed that Janice knew, or thought she knew, enough about what I was feeling to bring me some "help." Feeling like anyone's charity case is low on my favorite feelings list. I changed for bed and brushed my teeth. Crawling under the sheets, I opened the book and promptly fell asleep reading the table of contents.

The next day was Saturday. Following the morning commotion and

THE INVISIBLE WOMAN

a lunch with the neighborhood's five-year-olds, I made my first attempt to start the book. It would be nice to tell you that I put the kettle on for tea and curled up in my favorite chair by the fire. But the truth is, I walked right past the chaos in the kitchen where Jake was yelling at Tim amidst tears and drama, "You ate the Butterfinger that I was saving!" I walked right past my husband sitting on the floor in the living room carefully taking apart something that seemed to be broken. It occurred to me that he might be about to break it a little more completely, but I kept walking. I finally reached my sanctuary. I locked the bathroom door behind me and opened the book to read.

Knowing very little about great cathedrals, I began to get an education right away. A period of three centuries, from 1050 to 1350, several million tons of stone were quarried in France for the building of cathedrals and churches. "More stone was excavated in France during these three centuries than at any time in ancient Egypt. The foundations of the cathedrals are laid as deep as a Paris underground station and, in some cases, there is as much stone below ground as can be seen above."

Having had no idea about the size of those buildings, I was stunned. For example, the spire on the Strasbourg cathedral in France is the equivalent of a forty-floor skyscraper. Another French cathedral, Amiens, was built big enough for the entire population of the city, some ten thousand people, to gather together to attend a service. That didn't sound so impressive to me until the writer pointed out that in modern terms, this would mean building a stadium large enough to seat one million people in the heart of a city with a population of one million. Even the largest stadium in the world today only seats 240,000.

It would be many pages before I understood why Janice had brought me this book, but the subject was interesting enough to keep me reading until I got there. Then I read a sentence that began to make everything clear:

"Some of the architects and bishops behind a few of these great buildings are known, and much credit is given to them for their work, but *the vast majority of the labor, the masonry, the carpentry, the stained glass was all done by people whose names history will never reveal.*"

I flipped through the book quickly, scanning the pictures and the details. There were very few names. Time and again, scanning down under "builder," I found the word "unknown." The cathedrals were built primarily *by people whose names history will never reveal.*

As I read about the magnitude of what they accomplished, it seemed unfathomable to me that we would never know who they are. Although some have become famous, most have continued to stump history by their disappearance. Their masonry captured empty space and flooded it with light, creating an architectural triumph that had never before been accomplished. Shouldn't these people, perhaps some of them women, be applauded for the way their artistic workmanship left a beautiful mark on the history of the world?

I paused and thought, *Okay, Janice, I get this.* Janice was showing me anonymous greatness and how work can be done for other reasons than credit, proving that history can still shine on people's names we don't know.

But that was just the very beginning. For days I studied the pages and the photographs of the great cathedrals. I went back to the book

again and again. I read and reread whenever I could, carrying the book from room to room as I went about my business.

Many of these cathedrals took over a hundred years to complete. That sentence passed right by me the first time I read it. It was the second time before it dawned on me what that might mean. One hundred years was far more than one working man's entire lifetime, which meant that many builders devoted their whole lives to a work they would never see finished. Something resonated in me—*devoted their whole lives to a work they would never see finished.*

I tried to imagine the sorrow a medieval townsman must have felt in knowing this. He could only hope that his son or daughter would one day see the completed work to which he had given his life. Would this craftsman strain to see the finished structure with the eyes of his spirit, trying to imagine what the bricks would become? He must have, if only because he would need that vision to keep him inspired every day. When he looked around all he saw was rubble and dust and an endless amount of work to be done. And yet he kept working.

Maybe I don't have to say so, but suddenly the laundry felt much more manageable. The book was starting to give me a perspective I had not been able to find on my own. And I kept reading.

For the first time in history, the Gothic artist looked around at ordinary existence and elevated it into beauty. While many of these builders and workers were townspeople, there were also a large number of monks. But unlike earlier monks, who were preoccupied with intellectual life, *these monks regarded manual work as a form of prayer.* In other words, they decided it might actually be holy to get their hands dirty for God. They prayed with their tools and skills, which obviously paid off, since their work surpassed previous work in its excellence and beauty. Perhaps that happened because their efforts were deeply inspired and infused with a holy purpose never before given to the work of hands.

How had I heard of great cathedrals all these years, even seen pictures of them, but never read things like this?

One particularly moving story told of a very prominent man who went to visit a cathedral that was being built. He stopped to watch one

The Invisible Woman

of the workers, perhaps a monk. He saw the worker carving a tiny bird into the inside of a beam that would eventually be covered over by the stone roof. The man asked the worker why he was spending so much time and giving so much attention to something that no one would ever see. The builder never looked up. He never stopped carving as he replied, "Because God sees."

Years later, Martin Luther urged ordinary people—not just the clergy—to find the same perspective. He told the world that it was not the nature of work that made it holy. Milking a cow was no less holy than giving an offering. Luther believed that a housewife had as great a calling as a high priest, and that both should perform his or her work as though God alone were watching. Holiness comes from God and from the heart of the person doing the work, not from the work itself.

Someone must have been listening to Luther, because now, centuries later, we read of exquisitely carved statues hidden behind walls, visible only by reaching in with a mirror through holes in the plaster. It

seems that medieval artists walled up some of their best work because they believed God himself saw it, and they left it for God's eyes only. I was surprised to read that some of these works have only been discovered in the last century.

These medieval artisans played a game of holy hide-and-seek, which lasted for hundreds of years. Their work was not hidden by someone else; they hid their own work. And unlike me, they played this hide-and-seek on purpose. They weren't afraid that no one would find out what they'd done. The one who mattered most had already seen it.

A twelfth century cathedral-building monk named Theophilus, one of the few whom history has revealed, offers this explanation for his work and writings, "I have not written down my precepts for love of worldly praise, nor in hope of a reward here on this earth . . . I have wanted to supply the needs and help the progress of many men for the greater honor and glory of His name."

Theophilus had fully answered the question I was struggling to answer. He did not need people to see him. He was not looking for

worldly praise or a great reward. He was working for something far greater. God himself had bestowed meaning and significance on his work, and it was to God that he looked for praise.

These cathedrals were not built in easy times. Their architecture reflected the conflicts of their day, capturing the chaos and complexity of their medieval world, which interestingly is still reality in our world. The Gothic cathedrals express *"a cry of human suffering, as no emotion had ever been expressed before or is likely to find expression again. The delight of its aspirations is flung up to the sky. The pathos of its self-distrust and anguish of doubt, is buried in the earth as its last secret."* Aspirations flung up to the sky . . . anguish of doubt buried in the earth.

Looking at the pictures of cathedrals like Notre Dame and Chartres, I could see the tension in the style that the writer describes as "aspirations that are always upward yet ever anchored downward." This is a unique architectural style that demonstrates the weight of the effort, yet all the weight seems invisible to the eyes.

Of all the elaborate symbolism which has been suggested for the

Gothic cathedral, the most vital and most perfect may be that slender nervure, the springing motion of the broken arch, the leap downwards of the flying buttress—the visible effort to throw off a visible strain—never lets us forget that Faith alone supports it, and that, if Faith fails, Heaven is lost.

As I looked more closely at the pictures, I could see that the author was right. The spire seemed undaunted and oblivious to the forces pulling it down. In these real and magnificent structures, the visible is supported by the invisible—faith. And that raised another interesting question: if the invisible is lost, is everything lost?

How I have wanted to lose my invisibility! Perhaps I've never realized all the "visible" that it supports. I have viewed my daily life, anchored in the dirt of responsibilities and realities, as all there is. But like that spire, my heart is always straining, reaching and aspiring to more. These two pulls in opposite directions seem to exist together, and the cathedrals illustrate the intrinsic worth of this magnificent and terrible tension and clearly reveal the beauty in it.

I stopped to think about one last amazing picture. It was a photo of the upper chapel of Sainte Chapelle in Paris. Like a suspended jewel, this chapel is a dazzling display that, as the writer points out, seems to be lacking any visible support. Invisible builders created what looks like invisible support. Their building seems to reflect beautifully the hearts of those who were doing the building—hearts invisibly supported by faith.

The stained-glass windows of Sainte Chapelle hold enough colored pieces to illustrate eleven hundred biblical stories that are depicted there. These works of art were created by thirty master glaziers, all unknown, who labored for more than six years on just the windows. Fifteen times taller than they are wide, these jewel-like pictures illustrate the biblical stories that animated the glaziers' hearts and minds. They created, sacrificed, and worked invisibly, hoping and perhaps even boldly trusting that their work would bring glory and honor to God.

Near the end of the book, the writer expresses his belief that no cathedrals could be built in our lifetime because there are so few

THE INVISIBLE WOMAN

people who would be willing to sacrifice to that degree. It makes me wonder if there are fewer and fewer people who have a faith that can inspire such greatness. Some of these workers, like the anonymous stained-glass artists, had no idea of the impact their work would have as it played the role of picture book, becoming the first Bible some people ever saw. Many never saw their finished glass placed in its final home in the cathedral. But they must have known that when people looked through their windows they would see the world differently. So they sacrificed and created a bigger picture than they could fully see themselves.

My mind was trying to grasp just how much these builders had to teach me, to teach all of us. They definitely understood sacrifice in a way we no longer do. They believed enough in the greatness of their purpose to show up day after day at a job that they would never see finished, to work on a building that their name would never be on, trusting that by their selfless efforts they were making a lasting contribution to the world.

I closed the book and sat alone for some time. I wanted to hold it all in my heart. It was almost as if I heard God say, "Charlotte, I see you. You are not invisible to me. I see the sacrifices you make every day. I miss nothing. No act of kindness, no peanut butter sandwich made, no shoe selection is too small for me to notice and smile over. I see your tears of disappointment when you feel overlooked or when things don't go the way you want them to. But you are building a great cathedral, and you cannot possibly see right now what it will ultimately become. It will not be finished in your lifetime, and you will never be able to live there, but if you build it well, I will."

3.

Chapter Three

Love's Most
Beautiful Costume

chapter three

Love's Most
Beautiful Costume

I sat with my coffee at the kitchen table, looking outside at the little birdbath in our backyard. Mostly we get the little brown, common sparrows. Every once in a while we'll get a blue jay, but they're mean. Pretty to look at, they are noisy and barge right in, taking what they want with a lot of pushing and shoving; they strut around that little bath like they own it. There's a lot of drama when a jay is around, but mostly it's just the sparrows. There is one little guy with a bad foot, and he hops around the edge on one leg by himself. It seems he waits until the coast is clear to take his bath. I can only distinguish him because of his little hop.

Sitting and watching, I thought of the scripture, "Not a sparrow falls to the ground that God doesn't notice. So don't be afraid, aren't you worth more than the sparrows?" I thought about the question and how knowing and insightful it was. Maybe I really didn't believe I was worth so much or that my life mattered. Maybe I was afraid I would fall to the ground unnoticed. Yes, and end up with my picture on the back of a milk carton.

I thought about that little bird that the craftsman was carving into the beam. Remember, the one that would be covered over by the roof and no one but God would see? It had to be a sparrow! That must have been the message that the builder was carving into the beam. If he saw his work as prayer, perhaps that was his prayer as he was forming that little bird: *Father, help me remember that you see the sparrow, and that you see me too.*

He could never have known that hundreds of years later, I would read about his work in a book. He thought his offering was invisible to everyone but God. That builder will never know that his faithfulness to God in the twelfth century would reach my twenty-first century heart

and encourage me beyond measure. Or maybe he will. Maybe God will give him a glimpse of the way his inspired work has served to inspire me.

I sat at my table amidst the breakfast crumbs, mulling over the words of an old gospel song, letting the familiar words flood my heart with new meaning, "I sing because I'm happy. I sing because I'm free. His eye is on the sparrow, and I know he watches me."

If it wouldn't have been so corny, I might have called Janice and sung it to her. Maybe I would take her to lunch and try to explain the impact the book had made and was continuing to make on my life. While it doesn't seem very realistic to say everything seemed different, it wouldn't be honest to say anything else. I was and probably still am invisible to my family, and the jury remains out on Bonnie the mixed beagle, but I am not invisible to God. The great cathedrals were beginning to inspire my heart. I found myself being empowered in a very deep way by this new realization that God sees me, and I wanted to hold on to this new truth on the inside for a while. I kept thinking, *If God sees every little detail of my life, and I am not invisible to him, how will this make a difference?*

I carried the book around for weeks. I kept it with me in the laundry room, or lying around in the kitchen as a reminder. When I was cooking dinner I would see it there and be reminded of the builders or the stained-glass makers and the way they viewed their work. Standing over the stove, I began to whisper prayers that God would help me begin to see my own work in that same way.

In a bookstore one afternoon I saw a little notepad with a tiny pencil-drawn bird on it. I liked it immediately and bought it to put with the book so I could scribble down some of the things I was thinking. The first thing I wrote down was, "You may feel invisible in the world, but you are not invisible to God."

What would it mean to my everyday life if I could see the work that I do as a real form of prayer? What if I bowed my head over the laundry and said a prayer of blessing rather than my usual cursing? How could I see my role as a wife and the mother of two boys as though I were building a great cathedral? Would this change my day, or more to the point, my heart? How does one spread peanut butter as though it is a great offering to God? Will it spread more smoothly?

You may feel invisible in the world, but you are not invisible to God.

I definitely need the same strength my cathedral-building predecessors had in order to show up at my own building site without being discouraged, because I can't see the finished product at the end of the day, or week, or month. Exactly like that medieval townsman, most of what I see around me is under construction and unfinished, covered in a cloud of dust and surrounded by chaos. But looking back at history lets

me see things those craftsmen and women could not see. Having the long view reveals everything their sacrifices accomplished.

One of the monks, Abelard, quotes a schoolmaster from Chartres: "We are as dwarfs mounted on the shoulders of giants, so that we can perceive much more than they, not because our vision is clearer, nor because we are taller, but because we are lifted higher thanks to their gigantic height."

What height I have because I can stand on those builders' shoulders! The vista of history is hundreds of years more open to me than it was even to Abelard. With new eyes to see, borne on those strong shoulders, I am lifted higher. I continued to make my rounds with the book and notepad, writing down anything I needed to remember. I didn't want to be lifted to this great new height and then forget what I saw while I was up there.

It dawned on me that many of the female artists I respect the most have written poetry, songs, stories or painted canvases from an unseen place, trying to make their way in the world. Funny, being so aware of my

own invisibility, one would think I would have kept them in mind. Sylvia Plath, Maya Angelou, Janis Ian, Georgia O'Keefe, Flannery O'Connor, Carole King—all of these women have created art out of feelings of invisibility. Out of pain and perseverance, they have built or are still building their cathedrals in the world. In various forms they are shouting into the world, or whispering into our hearts, "We see you."

Like me, women who feel invisible don't automatically see others. I guess I concentrated so hard on my own invisibility that I was blind to anyone else's. I couldn't see all the other women around me who have similar feelings and share the same pain. But God sees. And although I *feel* invisible, I'm really not. This has opened my eyes to many other invisible people living, breathing, and struggling around me. The world has come alive with invisible people.

Once your eyes have been opened, you can't close them. The hymn "Amazing Grace" was written by John Newton, a slave trader whose eyes were opened. He described that grace, saying that once he'd been blind, but now he was able to see. That was amazing to him.

God saw him and then he could see everything around him. He finally saw the invisible slaves, and once he saw them, he could never *not* see them again.

I'm standing tall on the shoulders of giants and looking out across so much more of life than I ever have viewed before. In my field of vision are countless people I never noticed until I was convinced that God sees me.

I see a single mother in the grocery store. The baby is in the buggy finally cooing happily, but a little spit-up still remains on the left shoulder of Mom's blouse. She is holding the hand of a toddler, but no one is holding hers, as revealed by her bare ring finger. She buys a gallon of milk and quickly moves on. She has more errands to manage alone before she makes her way home to an empty house to change more diapers and spread out more Cheerios. She will cry tonight as sadness gets under the covers with her. After a full hard day, no one is there to hold her and whisper that everything will be all right. Being a single mother has made her invisible.

I see my neighbor Susan. An older African American woman, she feels invisible for reasons someone with my white skin would know nothing about. But I can see the way she is constantly bumped by all the people that never see her standing there, people who feel "safe" to say horrible things in her presence as if she isn't even there. She is bruised and sore from comments and careless words that hit her heart like thrown stones. The tunnel vision of ignorant people threatens to erase her from existence every day. And every single night she rubs the salve of forgiveness on her tender and sore soul. But her color makes her invisible.

I see a woman in the park walking with her child who has special needs. I feel her pain over the sightlessness of the world. People cannot fix their gaze on her child. Their clueless eyes look right past both of them. Her heart staggers under the weight of fear that her child will be marginalized in school because people cannot really see him. She sighs in frustration as she tries to cope with the child's lack of cooperation—a child who she understands

and hates at the same time. As the mother of a special-needs child, she's invisible.

I see a female soldier fighting for our country, afraid she'll be forgotten at home. With no way to communicate where she is or what she is being asked to do, she doubts herself. She wonders whether or not she's doing the right thing and questions whether she's making any difference. Day after day she fights a battle that, with the exception of breaking news sound bites and body counts, is pretty much invisible to the rest of the world. I feel her anguish over people who can't appreciate the freedom they have, or the high cost of keeping it. War has made her invisible.

I see a bald, thin woman rolling over in bed, desperately trying to sleep after "healing" drugs have forced her to empty the contents of her stomach for the forth time. Hopeful as ever, she calls herself a cancer "survivor." Although she is surrounded by love, the pain she is living with keeps her hidden from many of her closest friends. She is in her room, shades down and door closed, wondering why she has to go to

chemotherapy today when her friends are going to the museum. Cancer has made her invisible.

All the silent sacrifices, the hidden courage, the mustard seeds of faith, and the dogged determinations—none are invisible to God. If I see these women around me, with my limited vision, what must the panorama of heaven look like?

I wrote down on my little bird notepad, "Illuminate the sacrifices of others who are invisible to the world."

Sadly, the period of the great cathedrals ended for both the English and the French during the fourteenth and fifteenth centuries. Many attempts were made to revive the era, but the funds that were raised were never enough, and eventually people no longer responded to appeals to build houses for God. Somewhere along the way corruption had entered the scene, and excesses and other problems arose. The builders organized themselves into powerful guilds and ceaselessly defended their rights. The deep, uplifting faith of the twelfth and thirteenth centuries some-how faded, no longer inspiring the soul nor inflaming the heart.

Illuminate the sacrifices of others who are invisible to the world.

And how little I have relied on my own faith for strength! I am just beginning to come alive again as I discover how strong and intentional faith was for those builders, not to mention how essential it is for me.

Somewhere along the way, I managed to make God invisible in my life, placing him in the same position my family had put me. I didn't see what God was doing, so I treated him as if he wasn't there. I had it in

my mind that God was just supposed to answer my prayers (the butter God?) and then move out of the way and disappear. You would think that after knowing how it feels to be invisible I would know better than to trust only what I see. I'm pretty sure that makes me an invisible hypocrite. But just because I couldn't see God didn't mean God wasn't there, anymore than I am not there when my family can't see me.

It is so tempting to believe that I am missing out. Much in the world whispers that I am. TV sports figures and multi-million-dollar movie actors, glamorous supermodels, and powerful business executives all parade by as though they are living the summa cum laude of existence. It's hard not to trust what I see. Only faith can counter that misperception. Only faith convinces me that reality is so much more than the synthetic reality I see when I turn on the television. I will do well to keep my faith in what I can't see from being overshadowed by everything I see around me.

I have given a lot of thought to the role faith played in the building of the great cathedrals. Faith was the mortar between the stones; faith

was the lead securing the pieces of glass; and faith was the strength of the flying buttresses. The author's words came flooding back, "the visible effort to throw off a visible strain, never lets us forget that Faith alone supports it, and that, if Faith fails, Heaven is lost."

Objectively speaking, heaven is never lost, and faith doesn't fail; but when I fail to recognize faith, then heaven, is lost to me. Not the place of heaven, of course, but the perspective that eternity gives to my life today is lost or at least rendered powerless to give me any strength or hope. If the invisible is traded for only the visible, I will soon buckle under the strain.

I got my notepad and wrote another little note to remind myself, "Heaven may be the greatest purpose on earth."

Growing up, getting married, having children, maturing, gaining weight, losing sight—everything added up to erase my life. Invisibility was thrown over me like a blanket that I couldn't get out from under. But now that I am learning to trust that God really sees me, I'm seeing invisibility in a different way. Maybe disappearing can become a matter

of choice. Maybe I can use invisibility as a disguise for covert love operations. Maybe I can use anonymity as a means of not drawing attention to myself, and fade into the background whenever I need or want.

Perhaps invisibility is a gift, given to me for a greater purpose than I had previously seen. Like certain animals that can change their color or blend in to the environment when they are in danger, this quality may

Heaven may be the greatest purpose on earth.

have been given to me so I can love my family better, or to speak words of comfort to other invisible women.

In fact, there are some things I can't do unless I am invisible. I started to think about that medieval hide-and-seek that many of the artists played with their work and I was inspired. What could I hide in the lives of those I love if I used my invisibility? What could I leave on the earth that might never be discovered? What could I anonymously do for my family, for my friends, for humanity, or even for God?

One Saturday morning, I was making breakfast when Jake announced, "I have a secret admirer."

"I'm sure you have many, son," I smiled, scrambling eggs in a bowl.

"I found a candy bar in my backpack after recess."

"Wow, a whole candy bar?"

"Yep. I think it might be Emily; she knows I like Twix." And then he added, "And she smiles at me all the time."

"Could be, Jake; it's hard to tell when so many people like you," I winked.

"And two days ago, somebody's mother left cupcakes for our whole class."

"Really?"

"Yep. They had little birds on them, and they were good, too."

"I wonder who did *that?*"

He thought for a minute and shrugged. "I think it was Emily's mom."

"That's pretty nice." I smiled again as I put the eggs on the stove. "Maybe you should wash your hands before breakfast."

He hopped down from his chair and said, "It's cool to be secretly admired."

Yes, it is, I reminded myself.

While I will never be visible to everyone; I am finally able to see myself for the builder and woman that I am. I can stop searching for my reflection in others and allow God the opportunity to answer the question in my soul. My life really matters. These days I'm enjoying it thoroughly when someone doesn't see me. In fact I'm looking for new ways to disappear daily.

I put these words on my notepad, "Invisibility is not inflicted upon me; it is a gift to help me truly serve."

One night, late, Michael and I were lying in bed, about to fall asleep, when he said, "Thanks for taking Bonnie to get her shots yesterday. I know you really didn't have time to do that."

I smiled. "You never notice stuff like that."

"Yes, I do. I just never say anything about stuff like that."

I cautiously whispered, "Sometimes I wonder if you really see me."

He reached for my hand and said, "I don't always see what you *do*,

Invisibility is not inflicted upon me; it is a gift to help me truly serve.

but I always see *you*." We lay there in the dark and I could hear the smile in his voice as he tenderly added, "Even with the lights off." In that moment, I was glad the darkness hid the tear rolling down my cheek.

Do I want my family to see me and notice everything I do? Of course I do, but not if I have to *make* them see me. That's too high a price. I know many women who trumpet their own achievements, reciting them to anyone who will listen and sometimes to a few who won't.

"I do all the laundry by nine in the morning!"

"I have a hot meal on the table every night at five-thirty."

"I make sure my kids have all their schoolwork done before they turn on the television."

Some women take credit for everything that touches them, including their kids' successes and their husband's achievements. It's the only way they know to impress other people. Receiving the credit for every accomplishment becomes the basis of their identity, and it is a subtle form of idolatry.

But maybe you're asking, "Shouldn't I be noticed and seen? Don't I deserve to be loved and paid attention to?" In my heart these kinds of questions and other legitimate desires wrestle with the quietness of love and the beauty of invisibility. "I took the dog to the vet—me, Charlotte, the college graduate; the strong, capable lawyer who could be spending her time doing something else." What a noisy gong.

Many times I have wanted to make Michael's vision better, if only to sidestep the work I needed to do in my own heart. That is not to say that many men couldn't use some eye surgery to remove their sports cataracts or correct the shortsightedness that keeps them from being able to affirm and applaud their wives. But if I were able to find my deepest security in Michael's ability to see me, it's quite possible that I would never fully recognize the opportunity to depend on God for the greatness of a cathedral.

The deepest identity and worth that my heart longs for will never be found in human applause. Although it feels good most of

the time, it is far too short-lived. The deepest satisfaction of my heart is found in the faith to work and build and love for a greater purpose than my own.

When I see an unselfish, simple act of love, I am deeply moved. I am left speechless by the silent sacrifices love makes without ever drawing attention to itself. Often my hardened heart is reduced to liquid when I see a daughter wiping the drawn mouth of her parent, or a wife sitting by the bedside reading to a husband who can no longer see, or a friend helping a co-worker in a wheelchair get situated into an airplane seat. Through my tears, I want to stand and applaud the beauty of their sacrifice. It is a building in progress and it encourages me to keep going. Some people might be looking around to see who is watching them, or complaining about the task at hand, or even doing nothing instead of giving selflessly. I am fully convinced that invisibility is love's most beautiful costume, given only to its choicest of servants when they are really serious about serving.

Everyone—and I include myself—wants to be a servant until we're treated like one. I want to look like a servant, but not have to suffer. And if I have to suffer, I would like to be exalted for my servanthood. I have no idea how many years Mother Teresa worked invisibly in the streets of Calcutta before anyone ever knew her name, but I'm certain it was decades. When she came to renown, ironically her name was not the one that mattered. She walked among the poor, cloaked in humility, completely disguised as Jesus. Disappearing among the poorest of the poor, she made them visible with her quiet, strong love.

It is possible that the opposite of love is not hate or even apathy, but showy, self-serving acts. Talking or writing about how much you love, demanding your right to be loved, or being loud and brassy about the way other people don't love will never reveal love's truest essence. The greatest demonstrations of human love in history stand in direct opposition to such circus acts, in the way they are freely and quietly given. They humble us all, and by their power they change the world.

Invisibility is love's most beautiful costume.

And on my little notepad that was keeping my most important thoughts about this, right next to the little sparrow that only God sees, I wrote, "Invisibility is love's most beautiful costume."

THE INVISIBLE WOMAN

One day I was between walking upstairs to get something and going to the kitchen to return something, when I forgot what I was going to do in either place. I was standing in the living room like a total bump on a log when Tim, my oldest son, came walking by on his way upstairs. He looked at me strangely, tilted his head, and asked, "What are you doing?"

I was unable to offer any explanation other than, "I'm not sure." We stared at each other for a few seconds and then burst out laughing.

In that moment, Tim saw me. He looked me in the eyes, for no particular reason. I wasn't doing anything, performing any function, and he didn't need anything or even want to say anything. He just saw me standing there like an idiot, and it was funny to both of us. Of all the times to notice me, why then? He turned to go, and I could hear him laughing all the way up the stairs. It was sweet music to my invisible ears, melting away the fog of confusion that had settled between them.

Finally, last night I sat down with a pen, a nice piece of stationery, and a full heart.

Dear Janice,

You have no idea what The Great Cathedral book has meant to me. Beginning with your beautiful inscription, I devoured every page of the book. I first felt gratitude to you, dear friend, who knows me well enough to give me a book like this, and then moved to thanking God for loving me so well as to give me a friend like you.

It has been deep encouragement to my heart to learn that much of the great work in history has been done invisibly, endowed with a strength and purpose greater than the work itself. The builders of the cathedrals and their work have caused me to consider that the greatest purpose on earth must be connected to that which is beyond it. And God is showing me a way to live every day as though I believe it.

You've given me quite a gift. May it count for eternity.

With love from an invisible, cathedral-building woman, and your friend,

Charlotte

At times my invisibility still feels like an affliction. I still feel as though I might buckle under the weight of carrying so much responsibility. But then I think about the cathedrals, and my heart is shored up by the image of the flying buttress—throwing off visible strain by the strength of their design. I see the physical representation of so much yearning upward and grounding downward. And I know that I can survive another day. Maybe, like the cathedrals I have come to love, I'll make it another eight hundred years.

Invisibility is no longer a disease that is erasing my life. It is actually the hard cure for the disease of self-centeredness. It is the antidote to my stubborn pride. Many of these thoughts are still beyond my reach, but they lie within my hope for the future. Life still challenges me and invisibility still threatens, but I am able to remind myself, *It's okay that they don't know; it's all right that they don't see. God sees.*

Next Thanksgiving I don't want my son to tell his friends, "My mom gets up at four in the morning and bakes pies and hand-bastes a turkey for three hours and presses all the linens for the table." I don't

want his attention to be called to the things that I do. Those things mean nothing, and might even indicate that I've built a shrine, or some other not-so-great cathedral, in honor of myself. I just want him to want to bring his friends home often, and maybe to say something like, "You're gonna love it at my house. It's a great place to be."

I'm building a cathedral, but not *for* them, *in* them. And they will not see me if I'm doing it right. As a mother and a wife, I can be an extraordinary invisible builder, faithfully building what I cannot even see myself. Having set my sights so high, the foundation must go deep. I don't work for my husband and children; I work for God. And I am able to stand on the shoulders of giants who have gone before me and use what they have taught me to see things with a clarity that is not my own.

I'll keep building away, pouring my heart into this life, trusting that it is not in vain. I'll carve tiny birds into things that few eyes will ever notice. I will see my work as prayer, and trust that His eyes miss nothing. I will resist the temptation to live only in the now and keep reminding myself that I cannot see how wide the influence of my life could be,

nor the length of my possible legacy. Those are not for me to know. It is for me to keep building, and pray that long after I'm gone, my work will stand as a great monument to an even greater God. In the inspired words of Theophilis, "I have not written for love of worldly praise, nor in hope of a reward here on this earth . . . I have wanted to help the progress of many women for the greater honor and glory of His name."

Almighty God, who sees every sparrow, continue to teach me life's great lessons from the world's great cathedrals. Make me more invisible. Strengthen my heart to do the things that no one sees or appreciates, and to do them as unto you. Help me make personal sacrifices with no trumpet and no credit to myself. Let me be more invisible in you, so that real love may be more clearly visible. Let me allow humility to cloak my love at every opportunity. And if history never knows my name, may I have helped it know yours a little better. Allow me to be invisible, that the world might see you—the living God who sees and loves all invisible women.

Bibliography

Gimpel, Jean. *The Cathedral Builders*. New York: Grove Press, 1983.

Erlande-Brandenburg, Alain. *The Cathedral Builders of the Middle Ages.* United Kingdom: Thames & Hudson, 1995

Adams, Henry. *Mont St. Michel and Chartres*. Middlesex, England: Penguin Books, 1986

Yancey, Philip. *Rumors of another world*. Grand Rapids: Zondervan, 2003.

Ellison, Ralph. *The Invisible Man*. New York: Random House, 1952

Endnotes

CHAPTER 2

1. Page 33 – Quote that begins at the bottom of 33.
   The Cathedral Builders, p. 1

2. Page 34 – Quote at the bottom of 34.
   Cathedral Builders of the Middle Ages.

3. Page 42 – Theophilus quote. *The Cathedral Builders,* p.153. Public domain.

4. Page 44 – Quote that begins "The Gothic cathedrals express . . ."
   Henry Adams. *Mont St. Michele and Chartres,* p.359.

5. Page 44 – Top paragraph. Henry Adams. *Mont St. Michele and Chartres,* p.359.

CHAPTER 3

1. Page 54 – Matthew 10:29-31, *Holy Bible, New Century Version.*

2. Page 55 – Civilla D. Martin, "His Eye Is on the Sparrow," 1905.

3. Page 60 – Quote from Chartres. *The Cathedral Builders,* p. 36

4. Page 70 – First paragraph quote. Henry Adams. *Mont St. Michele and Chartres.*

5. Page 87 – Theophilus quote. Public domain.

Photo Credits

1. Page 4 – ©PhotoAlto Photography/VEER

2. Page 7 – ©Ryan McVay/Photodisc/Getty Images
   ©Stockbyte Photography/VEER

3. Page 11 – ©Anderson Ross/Photodisc/Getty Images

4. Page 13 – ©PhotoAlto Photography/VEER

5. Page 16 – Public domain

6. Page 20 – ©Royalty-Free/CORBIS

7. Page 32 – Public domain

8. Page 36 – Public domain

9. Page 37 – Public domain

10. Page 40 – Public domain

11. Page 43 – Public domain

12. Page 46 – ©Nicole Johnson, 2004

13. Page 48 – ©Nicole Johnson, 2004

14. Page 56 – Public domain

15. Page 57 – Public domain

16. Page 62 – ©Nicole Johnson, 2004

17. Page 69 – ©Nicole Johnson, 2004

18. Page 74 – ©Royalty-Free/CORBIS

19. Page 79 – Public domain

20. Page 82 – ©Alex L Fradkin/Photodisc/Getty Images

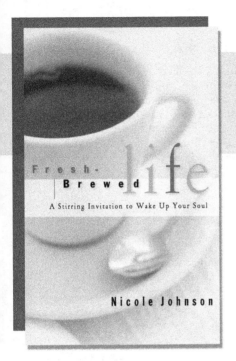

Fresh-Brewed *life*

*A Stirring invitation to
Wake up Your Soul*

God is calling us to wake up, to shout an enthusiastic "Yes!" to life just as we say yes to our first sip of coffee each morning. Nothing would please Him more than for us to live fresh-brewed lives, steeped in His love, filling the world with the marvelous aroma of Christ.

THOMAS NELSON
Since 1798

The Faith, Hope, and Love Trilogy

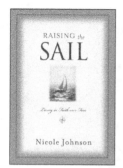

RAISING THE SAIL

Just as sailboats are made for the wind, women are made for relationships, and with both it takes faith to overcome the fear to let go and trust God's direction. Instead of frantically paddling or "motoring" our way through the seas of our emotional connections with each other, she challenges us to freely let go and trust the "Windmaker," God Himself, to help us find our way.

STEPPING INTO THE RING

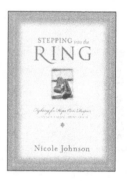

Where is the woman, old or young, who will not shed a tear but silently scream in her heart as she walks in these pages through the diagnosis of breast cancer and the devastation that ensues? While she focuses on the specific soul-chilling crisis, Nicole offers her readers broader insights for dealing with major losses of all kinds. She extends genuine hope and much-needed rays of light to those who are mired in hopelessness and despair.

DROPPING YOUR ROCK

You can express your moral outrage by joining the angry mob howling for a sinner to be stoned. But what if that sinner is your friend, and you would rather change her heart than shed her blood? We don't have to hurl the rocks we clutch in our judgmental hands. With tender words and touching photos, Nicole Johnson guides us toward the "flat thud of grace" that can change our lives when we drop our rocks and choose to love instead.

THOMAS NELSON
Since 1798

WOMEN OF FAITH

KEEPING A PRINCESS HEART
IN A NOT-SO-FAIRY-TALE WORLD
WITH CONVERSTION GUIDE

Every little girl grew up hearing the stories of "happily ever after," but finds it hard to believe that such a world still exists today. *Keeping a Princess Heart* is a deeply thoughtful exploration of the tension women feel between what they *long for* and what they *live with*. Women will discover how to hold on to their dreams as they take a deep, trusting dive into the wonderful world of fairy tales to reclaim a hidden treasure: a princess heart.

THOMAS NELSON
Since 1798